I0412569

Understanding the Needs of Elderly African Immigrants

Understanding the Needs of Elderly African Immigrants

A Resource Guide for Service Providers
in Central Minnesota

Komla Happy Ocloo

iUniverse, Inc.
Bloomington

Understanding the Needs of Elderly African Immigrants
A Resource Guide for Service Providers in Central Minnesota

Copyright © 2011 by Komla Happy Ocloo.

All rights reserved. No part of this book may be used or reproduced by any means, graphic, electronic, or mechanical, including photocopying, recording, taping or by any information storage retrieval system without the written permission of the publisher except in the case of brief quotations embodied in critical articles and reviews.

iUniverse books may be ordered through booksellers or by contacting:

iUniverse
1663 Liberty Drive
Bloomington, IN 47403
www.iuniverse.com
1-800-Authors (1-800-288-4677)

Because of the dynamic nature of the Internet, any web addresses or links contained in this book may have changed since publication and may no longer be valid. The views expressed in this work are solely those of the author and do not necessarily reflect the views of the publisher, and the publisher hereby disclaims any responsibility for them.

Any people depicted in stock imagery provided by Thinkstock are models, and such images are being used for illustrative purposes only.
Certain stock imagery © Thinkstock.

ISBN: 978-1-4620-1926-7 (pbk)
ISBN: 978-1-4620-1927-4 (ebk)

Printed in the United States of America

iUniverse rev. date: 06/22/2011

Acknowledgements

M y most obvious gratitude goes to God. This work would not have been possible without God's help. I want to acknowledge my loving wife Pauline, and my three wonderful daughters Wonder, Deborah, and Adjo Sika who support me in every way who were always behind me in every step of my school development.

Every one of them is special, and I cannot imagine doing this without their emotional and spiritual support. I wish to extend grateful appreciation to my advisor, Dr. Phyllis Greenberg. Her guidance and sense of humor were wonderful gifts to the completion of this book. Thank you, also, to Dr. Rona Karasik, Dr. Fred Hill, and Dr. Chucks Uguchuku for their ideas and contributions to this book. I am also grateful for all friends who gave encouragement and supported me to achieve this goal....

Table of Contents

Introduction

Over the last few decades, there has been a significant increase in the number African immigrants to the central Minnesota area (United States Bureau of the Census, 2005).The population of African immigrant elders age fifty-five and over (herein referred to as elder African refugees, elder immigrants, or African immigrant elders) has increased as a direct consequence of this rise in emigration. The most rapidly growing subgroups of the African immigrant population in central Minnesota are Somalis, Sudanese, and Ethiopians (USBC, 2005). According to the Bureau of the Census (2005), the majority of these African immigrants are refugees who cross national boundaries in search of safety. Among these ethnic groups, members of minority groups tend to flee because they fear persecution. In countries experiencing civil war, fighting among factions has resulted in the death, dislocation, and starvation of thousands. This had led many Africans to move to the United States in search of a second chance. Most of these immigrants face many challenges in adapting to a new culture, language, and climate, and understanding cultural values, norms, taboos, traditions, and patterns of interaction in their adopted country (United Nations, 2006). Elderly immigrants are often more challenged simply by nature of their age and the inertia of a long-established lifestyle.

People in Africa, as in other parts of the world, have a need to maintain their personal, spiritual, and religious values, which have come from teachings in the realm of Christianity, Islam, and other traditional tribal cultures.

The goal of this book is to provide information on the religion, spirituality, and culture of African elder immigrants so that government agencies, social organizations, and faith communities in central Minnesota can better serve the needs of these new arrivals. This resource guide will serve as an initial step in focusing attention on the challenges, strengths, problems, and possible solutions that affect this population.

The guide will be useful for providers in many settings, including healthcare, legal services, financial guidance, and education. By focusing on elder immigrants' cultural, religious, and spiritual needs, this project aims to provide a voice for this underserved population. The literature review that follows will help service providers to understand the problems and background of elderly African immigrants in central Minnesota.

Literature Review

A United States Bureau of the Census report (2006) showed that 13 percent of the overall population of central Minnesota was from Africa. Most of these individuals have come to the central Minnesota area as refugees from civil strife in Somalia, Ethiopia, Sudan, and Liberia (USBC, 2006). Somali immigrants comprise 7 percent of the overall central Minnesota population, and they are the largest group of African immigrants in central Minnesota (USBC, 2000). War, political strife, famine, flood, and drought forced more than one million Somalis to seek refuge in neighboring countries such as Kenya and Ethiopia. Most Somalis and Sudanese who now live in central Minnesota came there directly from refugee camps (United Nations, 2006).

A variety of economic, political and social factors contributed to the migration of African people from their native countries since 1990 (Drachman, 1995; Dyal & Dyal, 1981; Kohls, 1996). Many Africans sought to escape from political turmoil and persecution (United States Department of Justice, 1993). The majority of African immigrant elders were forced to flee from their homelands to avoid religious or political persecution, to escape from natural disasters such as floods or droughts, or to avoid the ravages of war (Allen, Cochrane, Dean, & Greene, 1989). Allen et al. (1989) argue that the common denominator among the African immigrant cultures is the involuntary nature of their migration and the hardship and suffering associated with it. The term "refugee" has been used to describe people migrating under these circumstances (Allen et al., 1989).

Economically, Africa is dependent on its natural resources (United Nations, 2005). Struggles to control natural resources such as oil, gold, cotton, diamonds, and hard-rock minerals have played key roles in civil wars in Africa (United Nations, 2005). When civil wars flare up in Africa, they are invariably fought along ethnic lines. This does not mean that the ethnic differences are causing the conflict (United Nations, 2005). However, they have been a factor in creating the economic situation from which refugees eventually flee.

Immigrants experience a tremendous amount of stress during the process of relocation (Dyal & Dyal, 1981; Padilla, 1980). Richardson (1987) points out that migration is a developmental process encompassing various tasks and demands. The following focuses on three aspects of acculturation: language, culture shock, and stress and depression. These three topics explain some of the challenges that African immigrant elders in central Minnesota face.

Recent data indicate that approximately 670,000 persons from Africa age sixty and over entered the United States as legal immigrants between 1988 and 1998 (Immigration and Naturalization Service, 2000). A number of communities, including central Minnesota, have experienced significant growth in African elderly populations (USBC, 2000).

One of the cultural barriers facing immigrants is acquiring proficiency in the English language. "Language use and ability limits the individuals, groups, and organizations with which one can interact," (Born, 1980, p. 91). Born (1980) and Blythe (1994) explain that language acquisition is particularly important for immigrants when the adopted society is skewed toward a single dominant language. In the United States, a person who does not speak English proficiently is potentially limited in his or her efforts to obtain schooling, employment, and social and health services (Born, 1980).

According to Esposito (1998), "language use and ability acts as a vehicle for supporting the unique cultural identity of those who speak that language, and acts as a barrier to out-group interaction." As a source and support of cultural identity, language use reinforces ethnic identity and group cohesion, promoting well-being while encouraging adherences to traditional norms and values that shape behavior (Jacob, 1994). These norms and values include those relating to gender roles, intergenerational obligation, and status of elders, among others (Jacob, 1994).

Getui, Holter, and Zinkuratire (2001) argued that the retention of native language among immigrants forms a shield against assimilation. This shield is far reaching, extending to issues of cultural identity, norms, and values. It also has implications for socioeconomic success (Getui et al., 2001). The reality is that language, cultural barriers, and misunderstandings can get in the way of effective communication and create complications for some African immigrants in their new communities. It is important for service providers, educators, trainers, and other human-resources professionals to gain a better understanding of and sensitivity to language barriers. Life in a new land is especially trying for African immigrants. They find themselves far away from their homelands, facing language barriers which are an obstacle to constructive interaction with service providers. For non-English-speaking African immigrants, effective social support connection may be limited to fellow members of their ethnic group. Older African immigrants with needs related to health care, financial assistance, and education may entirely depend on English interpreters.

African elders with poor English language skills may be more likely than those with adequate English skills to live with other community groups as opposed to living independently. Living with a person from another ethnic group could help immigrants improve their English skills (Born, 1980).

Culture Shock and
Cross-Cultural Adjustment

According to Collins, Kayser, and Tourse (1994), the term "culture shock" has become familiar to the majority of people around the globe, but a clear understanding of its meaning and import is much less common. Drachman (1995) described culture shock as primarily an emotional reaction that follows from not being able to understand, control, and predict another's behavior. This theme is also mentioned by Born (1980), who states that culture shock is a stress reaction, resulting from uncertainty in achieving emotional and physical rewards. According to Collins, Kayser, and Tourse (1994), culture shock is defined as difficulty adjusting to a culture markedly different from one's own. Culture shock occurs when immigrants' cultural clues, the signs and symbols which guide social interaction, are stripped away (Canedy, 2002). Adults feel like children again, creating a loss of dignity and a heavy need for dependence (Born, 1980). The reason some immigrants feel like children again is because their cultural identity suffers some sort of rejection or intolerance. This causes an immigrant person to feel inferior. This rejection also forces some immigrants to assume that their own culture is not good, and drives them to pretend to be something they are not in order to fit in, which can cause chaotic misunderstandings between themselves and the society they have to fit in with.

Longatan (2008) argues that culture shock is presenting a clear unmistakable impression from a common understanding of emtional disturbing. For example, African immigrant elders entering the United States, particularly in the central Minnesota area, may be shocked by many new experiences: the lifestyle, the speed and complexity of automobile traffic, the weather, the housing, the food, and the language (Collins, Kayser, & Tourse, 1994). Culture shock is a process of learning to live in entirely new ways, among people with entirely different lifestyles and ways of expressing themselves (Longatan, 2008).

The process of adjustment can be very painful, depending on a number of factors, including the difference between the home culture and the new one (Longatan, 2008). This adjustment can be both scary and exhilarating. The immigrant has to adjust every detail of life: whether and how to shake hands, how to eat, how to get around, what to wear, and how to behave in the simplest social interactions, such as what gestures to make or which questions to ask (Born, 1980).

African immigrant elders are sometimes surprised to find that cultures are not the same. Ordinary life becomes a series of tasks that can become intimidating (Kohls, 1996). It may be months or years before the newcomer begins to feel settled and competent at getting by in the new country. At first, negative feelings may be overwhelming: homesickness, frustration, strangeness, and the feelings of not knowing what is going on and how to cope (Kohls, 1996). African immigrant elders in central Minnesota often experience depression, or feelings that that life is no longer worth living. Depression can cause difficulty sleeping, flashes of irritation and temper, and doubt or suspicion about the host culture and population. These feelings are a very natural part of the adjustment process. No one can escape completely from culture shock (Longatan, 2008).

Overall, the process of cultural adjustment has been shown to be an important component of living in a new country. African immigrant elders who do not know or realize that some negative feelings are a part of culture shock may blame the host culture or people, taking on a negative attitude toward them that may never lift (Drachman, 1995). Others may blame themselves and take refuge in inappropriate behavior. The African immigrant elders who recognize the process of culture shock can give themselves time to let their perceptions gradually settle down, and then make a better assessment of the situation after the adjustment period is over (Longatan, 2008).

With care and patience, African immigrant elders can come to appreciate the foreign culture of the United States. Some African elders immerse themselves totally in the new culture, becoming fully "bicultural," while others hold back, maintaining their home identity while adopting and appreciating some new foods, holidays, customs, and friendships (Bloom & Fisher, 1982). No one is condemned to stay in culture shock forever; allowing for an adjustment period makes it easier to be open to the host culture (Collins, Kayser, & Tourse, 1994; Longatan, 2008). The following section will explore the stresses facing African immigrant elders living in a new country.

Stress and Depression Management

According to Perls and Silver (1996), "stress refers to a state of tension produced by pressures or conflicting demands with which the person cannot adequately cope" (p. 43). Perls and Silver also state that depression is a common mental disorder that leads to a depressed mood, loss of interest or pleasure, feeling of guilt or low self-worth, disturbed sleep or appetite, low energy, and poor concentration.

The literature suggests that controlling stress can reduce the risk of diseases such as heart attack and strokes, and can improve the immune system, which affects longevity (Nawwab, 1992). In addition, the literature suggests that prolonged stress is associated with sleep disturbances, increased health problems and an overall negative effect on everyday life (Perls & Silver, 1996). Depression is a disease. The risks among elderly immigrant can include irritability, sleep problems, feeling empty, helpless, or bored because they are disconnecte or facing challenges in a new country.

African Belief Systems

L imited attention has been paid to African immigrants by researchers, although they are a particularly vulnerable population (Adamo, 2000; Mbiti, 1990). More than 680 million people live in Africa, and the population of the continent is rapidly expanding. Even so, the peoples of Africa currently make up only 10 percent of the world's population. Africa is the second largest continent by land area, but its population density in some regions is rather low. This is due in part to the Sahara Desert, which occupies one-fourth of Africa's landmass and is largely not suitable for habitation. In those areas of Africa that can support agriculture, the population density is higher and is closer to the world average (United Nations, 2006). The peoples of Africa belong to several thousand different ethnic groups. Each ethnic group has its own distinct language, traditions, arts and crafts, history, way of life, and religion. Africa can be divided into five regions: North Africa, West Africa, Central Africa, East Africa, and Southern Africa. Each of these cultural and geographic regions is different from the others in many ways.

The philosophy or value system of Africans provides some background to understanding their immigration experience. Most Africans believe in a supreme being who controls the natural order of things (Mbiti, 1990). Some Africans believe in spirits or spiritual beings who work in concert with the supreme being (Mbiti, 1970), and much of African philosophy is life-centered and is expressed in prayers, invocations, and praises (Parachin, 1994). This focus on life is seen in prayers for obtaining life, restoring life, and preserving life from impending dangers; in prayers for recovery from illness; and in prayers for making life more abundant (Adamo, 2000). Although many Africans have embraced major Western and Eastern religious traditions, strong indigenous cultural and religious beliefs, rituals, and values permeate their self-understanding and celebration of life (Adamo, 2000; Parachin, 1994).

The Ethics and Morals of African Religion

The ethics and morals of African religiosity are embedded in values, customs, traditional laws, and taboos (Ben-Jochannan, 2002; Getui et al., 2001; Mbiti, 1970) Serious moral offences in Africa include disrespect or rudeness toward elderly people; sexual transgressions such as incest, rape, and intercourse with children; adultery; murder; stealing; robbery; telling lies; deliberately causing bodily or property harm; and the use of sorcery and witchcraft (Ben-Jochannan, 2002). On the other hand, kindness, friendliness, truthfulness, politeness, generosity, and hospitality are part of Africans' daily life. In addition, hard work, caring for the sick or elderly parents, respect for elderly people, and protection of children and women are virtues that earn praise and admiration in African communities (Getui et al., 2001). Mbiti, (1970) argues that in most Africa cultures a supreme being is understood to be watching over the moral life of the community, society, and humankind. Per Mbiti, from time to time, the supreme deity may punish the society or give warnings through calamities, epidemics, drought, war, and famine. The home and the community instill moral teaching, generally from the older to younger members, through examples (Getui et al., 2001). Stories, proverbs, and taboos are employed in the teaching of morals as well as for entertainment. At rare, auspicious, and unexpected moments, elders share their fascinating life experiences: a grandfather or grandmother reminiscing about their childhood in Togo (West Africa); grandparents remember life as shepherds; and telling stories under the palabre tree to their children and grandchildren. They share exciting stories while, some of the children play drums and sing traditional songs. Such people have something important to share. But all too often, experiences shared by voice die with the teller because they are not written down or recorded.

Christianity in Africa

C hristianity's presence in Africa probably began during the earthly ministry of Jesus Christ two thousand years ago (Kinkupu, 2005). The New Testament mentions several events in which Africans were witnesses to the life of Christ and the ministry of the Apostles. The Gospel of Luke records that a Cyrenian was compelled to bear the cross for Jesus, prior to Jesus's crucifixion. Cyrene was located in North Africa. The book of Acts records that, on the day of Pentecost, Egyptians and Cyrenians were among the crowd, and heard the Apostles proclaim the Gospel in their native languages. Acts also records the conversion of an influential Ethiopian eunuch to Christianity. Acts further tells that, following the Apostles' missionary journey to Cyprus, new converts from Cyprus and Cyrene preached the new religion to the Greeks of Antioch.

The spread of Christianity throughout Egypt and Northern Africa was rapid and intense, despite the prevalence of false teachings and persecution. Some religious scholars believe that Christianity was introduced to many Africans in the Egyptian city of Alexandria. Reportedly, the city boasted a very large Jewish community.

North Africans were the first Africans to receive and embrace the Gospel of Jesus Christ. The early Church in North Africa went through severe persecution. Many significant leaders of the faith emerged from the early African Church. Persecutions in Egyptian cities resulted in the dispersion of Christians to the hinterland. Egyptian churches spread the Gospel in Coptic, an Egyptian language, and planted churches throughout the interior of Egypt. Christianity in the region was weakened by theological and doctrinal controversies.

At the start of the seventh century of the Common Era, the Coptic Church had established itself as Egypt's national church and had penetrated every region of the country. The Church in North Africa did not grow as quickly as other Christian sects because the Latin language was used in services and literature, rather than the language of the people.

An influx of Muslims into Africa during the Middle Ages resulted in an exponential increase in Islamic converts, which forced many African Christians to flee to Europe. Missionary efforts by the Roman Catholic Church and European Protestant churches reclaimed some of the African continent for Christ.

Christianity was introduced in sub-Saharan Africa during the fourteenth and fifteenth centuries, and then reintroduced in the nineteenth. Although an imported religion, Christianity is growing markedly in Africa (Kinkupu, 2005). Christianity came to Africa before it reached Europe, and it was already in Africa long before European and American missionaries began to preach the Christian faith in other parts of the world (Geffre, 2006). According to Eloi (2006), Christianity in Africa is expressed differently across cultures.

Doctrinal Enculturation

D octrinal enculturation is the proclamation of faith, and the task is finding a way to introduce new ideas of expressing it in relation to cultural contexts in Africa Christianity. It is important not to separate the Christian doctrine from the ethical dimension of the Gospel or from enculturation (Kinkupu, 2005).

Although the majority of African immigrants to central Minnesota are Muslims, a significant percent of the new arrivals are Christians (USBC, 2005), mostly coming from East Africa (and some parts of West Africa). The differences between the practices of Christianity in Africa and in the United States present a formidable challenge for both immigrants and those who organize worship and related programs.

In Africa, Christianity is typically practiced in a vocal and expressive way (Kinkuku, 2005). The practice generally includes extensive clapping, singing, and dancing. These cultural elements have been incorporated into the practice of Christianity in many parts of Africa.

According to my own observations as a Christian minister, the typical Christian African immigrant in the United States and specifically in central Minnesota suffers from a deprivation of these active cultural elements in their practice of Christianity. Most American church services are rigidly structured and devoid of the participatory patterns characteristic of services in Africa. These differences may cause some spiritual culture shock, the potential for which Christian service providers should be aware. African immigrants have brought along with them their cultures and languages. It is clear that spiritual enculturation of African elders in central Minnesota is still a field which churches must look to for their future to fill the gap of the spiritual shock. Most elderly African Christians do not speak English well but worship in churches without interpreters. Per my own experience as a Christian immigrant, we can minimize spiritual shock if immigrants are allowed to worship in their own language and culture. In this way, Christian churches will also become cultural centers, transmitting cultural heritage to the next generation.

A lack of sensitivity about language and culture in American Christian churches, especially in central Minnesota, can be a source of stress for African elderly immigrants. In contrast, most

Muslims immigrants worship in the Arabic language, regardless of their geographic location.

Understanding Islam in Africa

With the Islamic cultural world being centered in the Middle East, it is often overlooked that the majority of the world's Muslims are in Asia, and that Islam predominates or is strongly represented in more than two-thirds of the African continent (Abou El Fadl, 2002). In addition to dominating Northern Africa, among Saharan and West African nations, Muslims are the majority of the population in Gambia, Guinea, Mali, Mauritania, Senegal, Chad, and Sudan. They form 25 to 50 percent of the populations of Burkina Faso, Ivory Coast, Nigeria, and Sierra Leone (United Nations, 2000). In East Africa, Muslims form a significant percentage in Kenya and Tanzania (27 percent), and they are a 99 percent majority in Somalia (United Nations, 2000). To better understand the lives of African immigrants to central Minnesota, we will undertake a sketch of the historical background of Islam, and the five pillars of the Islamic faith.

According to Islamic belief, Mohammad, a forty-year-old merchant of the Quraysh tribe in Mecca (in what is now Saudi Arabia), was commanded by the angel Gabriel to recite the messages of Allah—which is the Arabic name for God (Ben-Jochannan, 2002). Gabriel told Muhammad that humankind had lost sight of Allah's previous messages to earlier prophets Adam, Abraham, Moses, Noah, Solomon, and Jesus, among others; and that Mohammad was to spread Allah's message to all people so that mankind would know how to live, how to show respect for Allah, and how to prepare for the judgment day (Esposito, 1998).

The five pillars of the Islamic faith represent its most basic beliefs and practices. They are derived from the immutable source of the Islamic religion, the Qur'an (Esposito, 1998; Hussain, Olson, & Qureshi, 1984). Over time, different communities developed different interpretations of the Islamic faith. Variations of religious practice are often the result of the fusion of differing systems of belief. These variations usually coexist and rarely violate the unchangeable tenets of the faith (Esposito, 1998).

The Shahada (Testament of Belief)

The first pillar, the Shahada, or testament of belief, asserts the uncompromising monotheism of Islam, continuing the tradition of monotheism begun by Judaism and continued with Christianity (Ahmed, 1986). Tawheed, which means "there is no deity but Allah," is set forth in the first part of the testament: *la Allah ila Allah*. (Abou El Fadl, 2002; Abu-Lughod, 1989). The Holy Book, the Qur'an, was revealed to the prophet Mohammad, who existed in the realm of humanity, and is distinguished from Jesus Christ, who is believed by Christians to be divine (Hussain et al., 1984).

Ideally, the Shahada is the first thing that a Muslim child should have uttered in its ear and the last that a dying person should hear (Abu-Lughod, 1989). Parents may begin to teach their children how to speak by repeating the Shahada. The Shahada is recalled with each of the five daily calls to prayer, and is an ever-present reminder of the unity and oneness of God (Azoy, 2003).

Salat (Prayer)

P rayer in Islam repeats basic elements of testimony of belief, which are repeated in the call to prayer by the muezzin, who historically stood atop the minaret of the local mosque calling the faithful to prayer five times daily (Hussain, et al., 1994). "Prayer in a mosque in the direction of Mecca began among the earliest Muslim communities in Arabia" (Hussain et al., 1994, p. 101). Muslim prayer became ritualized around the following necessary steps: ablution, intention, bowing or bending forward, and prostration (Abu, 1995). Purification before prayer involves first the cleansing of the mind and then the washing of specified body parts including the face, hands, mouth (unless fasting), feet, and forehead (Abu, 1995).

According to Hussain et al. (1994), prayer is obligatory for all Muslims who have reached puberty. Of course, many younger children pray well before the age of puberty. Prayer is performed respectfully; those who pray do not wear shoes. Communal prayer in the mosque is considered a higher form of prayer, because it is collective and involves the broader Islamic community. Friday prayer is congregational and is led by an imam (Hussain et al., 1994 p. 83).

Sawn (Fasting)

A lthough the practice of Islam is intensely personal and individual, its rituals are highly public and collective (Abou El Fadl, 2002). The observance of the annual fast during the month of Ramadan, the ninth month of the Islamic calendar, begins when the new moon is seen. The month of fasting commemorates God's revelation of the Qur'an to Muhammad (Abu-Lughod, 1989; Ahmed, 1986).

During the Ramadan fast, avoiding food and drink from sunrise to sunset for one lunar month is obligatory for adult Muslim men and women, with only the young, the infirm, pregnant women, and travelers exempted (Abou, 2002; Abu, 1995). One mark of the maturing adolescent is the decision to begin to fast, the timing of which is a matter of personal choice (Abou, 2002).

Zakat (Almsgiving)

Zakat is the religious responsibility of every Muslim to share with fellow Muslims in need through charitable offerings (Ellison, 1983). Zakat in the form of an alms tax has been mandated by the government in certain Islamic republics, such as Sudan and Somalia (Ellison, 1983).

Zakat is a form of worship, as well as an act of thanksgiving and service to the community (Azoy, 2003). A religious tax, usually about 2-3 percent of one's accumulated wealth or assets, is expected (Azoy, 2003). Compliance with zakat is predicated upon the recognition of the injustice of economic inequity and the responsibility of Muslims everywhere to assist one another and the faith in a material way. One of the purest forms of zakat is aid given anonymously to someone in need (Abou, 2002; Azoy, 2003).

Performance of the Hajj

The pilgrimage to the Muslim holy places of Mecca and Medina is a religious duty that every Muslim is asked to perform at least once (Abou El Fadl, 2002). The focus of the pilgrimage is the Ka'ba, the small stone building in which one finds the black stone that the angel Gabriel gave to Abraham as a symbol of God's covenant with Abraham's son, Ishmael, and by extension with the Muslim community (Azoy, 2003). The Ka'ba was already a place of pilgrimage in pre-Islamic times. Tradition tells of Muhammad triumphantly entering Mecca after his prophecy and announcing his intention to cleanse the Ka'ba of its polytheistic idols and restore it to the worship and veneration of the one true God (Esposito, 1988).

When making the ambulation of the Ka'ba, pilgrims may touch or kiss the black stone, as did the prophet in his pilgrimages (Azoy, 2003; Esposito, 1988). According to some traditions, the black stone is the sole remnant of the original place of worship built by Abraham and Ishmael. "The stone has no devotional significance and is not an object of worship itself, consistent with the uncompromising monotheism of Islam" (Nawwab, 1992, p. 30). On the third day of the hajj, many pilgrims slaughter a sheep or goat to commemorate Abraham's willingness to sacrifice his son to God, a belief shared by Jews, Christians, and Muslims; and to symbolize Islam's basic tenet of submission to God's will (Callaway & Creevy,1994; Canedy, 2002).

The Role of Spiritual Leaders in African Religion

According to Buono, Urciuoli & De Leo (1998), spirituality can be defined as seeing a person as being composed of three separate parts: body, soul, and spirit. Buono, et al. (1998) suggest that an ecumenical, cross-cultural, and holy approach to "spirituality" is needed. Buono argues that "it is not the soul that seeks integration in holiness of life, but the whole person, body, spirit, mind, will, emotions, individual and social, male and female." (p. 83)

Spiritual leaders play unique roles in the lives of African immigrant elders. This section will focus on two facets of spiritual leadership: faith and compassion. These two concepts demonstrate the part that spiritual well-being could play in giving African immigrant elders a sense of making a difference, the feeling that one's life has meaning.

Health, Aging, and Faith Practice

Faith is considered one of the primary lifestyle categories in working with immigrant elders (Parachin, 1994). Faith may be referred to as religion or spirituality. In discussion of issues confronting African immigrant elders in central Minnesota, "spirituality," "religion," and "faith practice" are used interchangeably (Parachin, 2000). "Religion is defined as a unified system of practices and beliefs in spiritual beings relative to sacred things that are set apart and held in awe, that unites the believers into a moral community such as church, synagogue, or mosque" (Winter,

2000, p. 104). Faith practices have significant impact upon health, affecting levels of stress, depression, heart disease, and emotional problems (Buono, et al., 1998; Hickson, Housley, & Wages, 2000; Koenig, 2000; Parachin, 1994; Perls & Silver, 1996; Winter, 2000).

The literature suggests that faith practices become more important as people age (Buono, et al., 1998; Hickson et al., 2000; Koenig, 2000; Parachin, 1994; Perls & Silver, 1999; Winter, 2000). Elders may wish to practice their religion more frequently. African immigrant elders' relationship to spiritual development and faith practice may be tied to their particular cultural background. Research indicates that religiosity is more prevalent in people over the age of sixty-five (Winter, 2000). Some African immigrant elders participate in religion weekly, and three-quarters of them seek God's will through prayer (Buono, et al.,1998; Hickson et al., 2000). Most African immigrants aged sixty-five and older say their religious beliefs are a very important influence in their lives (Perls & Silver, 1996). According to my personal experience, the majority of African immigrant elders living in central Minnesota—Muslim or Christian—have strong ties to their faith communities. Research finds that approximately 33 percent of the world's population believes that at some time in their lives they have had a remarkable healing experience (Perls & Silver, 1996; Winter, 2000). In addition, within this group, 72 percent attribute that healing to God or a higher power (Hickson et al., 2000).

Research indicates that many religious people are physically healthier, lead healthier lifestyles, and require fewer health services (Koenig, 2000). For instance, studies done at the Harvard medical school indicate that frequent prayer, which is a part of most religions' beliefs and practices, can lower blood pressure and reduce pain in cancer patients (Collins, Kayser, & Tourse, 1994). Other research has found that those people who attend church, synagogue, or mosque regularly have lower levels of immune-system substance associated with stress (Perls & Silver, 1996).

Life Experience and Faith

The emotional implications of religious beliefs are powerful. Faith can help elderly people deal with life's circumstances (Hickson et al., 2000). This is also true for African immigrant elders. Finally, according to research by Perls & Silver (1996), another aspect of faith is that being part of God's plan is a key issue of African immigrant elders' spirituality and self-concept, encouraging them to face their new challenges in central Minnesota.

Although there may be many outcomes of faith practice, the literature supports the notion that religious beliefs can positively affect elderly people (Koenig, 2000). Faith and belief in a greater being may enhance African immigrant elders' life process physically, mentally, emotionally, or spiritually (Buono, et al. 1998; Hickson et al., 2000).

Implications for Practice

The literature shows strong relationships between and among variables such as culture, religion, and spirituality, suggesting that service providers ought to be aware of these interactive processes when working with the African immigrant elder population. Providers need to be sensitive to those conditions that enhance African immigrant elders' cultural, religious, and spiritual well-being. Ellison (1983) suggests that within the course of a therapeutic relationship, cultural, religious, and spiritual well-being can be positively affected (Hickson et al., 2000). Maher (1999), asserts that interventions to improve spiritual well-being are as essential as interventions directed to improving physical and emotional health.

Culture, religion, and spirituality are central to the life of African elder immigrants. This underscores the need for the development of a strong social network for African immigrants. Padilla, Alvarez, & Lindholm (1986) demonstrated that the most stressful phase of acculturation for African immigrants is evaluation of their proper role within the host society and subsequent to that, feelings of not belonging. Service providers may need to pay greater attention to their approaches to a variety of cultural and spiritual topics as they work with African elders.

The worldviews of African elders must be respected as they evolve in a new host culture. Mbiti (2000) notes that an African's identity is found in the community's identity. African elders are viewed as a part of or an extension of the environment because of the belief that everything is functionally connected. Self is viewed as part of interdependent relationships (Winter, 2000).

Elder Africans bring with them a unique cultural perspective. Service providers can use the second part of this book, a resource guide on the culture, philosophy, religion, and spirituality of African immigrant elders, to learn to provide more culturally competent services. Cultural competence encourages those needing help to learn to function in a larger culture and, at the same time, to appreciate their own sociocultural context. Service providers need to ask what constitutes spiritual life for African elders, why certain beliefs carry important meanings for some people, and what variations exist across African cultures. Service providers can explore with African immigrants the changing and evolving aspects of their spiritual well-being. Supporting the integration of creative spirituality requires understanding how people practice and think about religion. A better understanding of elders' spiritual needs is a big step toward the enactment and implementation of appropriate programs and policies for the African immigrant elder populations.

The role of service providers in empowering African elders has been documented (Allen et al., 1989). Service providers need to support African immigrants and explore with them those aspects of their lives that enhance their well-being. Attending to these concerns requires that service providers be self-aware, appreciate challenges as time- and culture-bound, and receive supervision and training when working with African immigrants. Finally, as new issues emerge, there is an urgent need for service providers to develop empirically based practices with African populations (Bloom & Fischer, 1982; Blythe, Briar, & Tripodi, 1994; Collins, Kayser, & Platt, 1994). As the nature and needs of African immigrant populations change, so must the focus of providers' efforts to deliver services. The delivery of services is intricately intertwined with policy and practice implications.

The successful integration of African immigrant elders into American culture depends on their post-migration experience. Communication skills, educational attainment, awareness of the new host culture, religion, and spiritual well-being are important variables that interact to enhance the well-being of elders. The development of research on these topics is only a beginning toward understanding the complexity of the cross-cultural transition and acculturation processes for African immigrant elders in central Minnesota.

Methods

In preparing this resource guide, I talked to many elderly refugees from many parts of the world, especially African elderly immigrants in central Minnesota. The goal of this guide is to help service providers, agencies, organizations, faith communities, and others who encounter elderly immigrants better understand the challenges African elderly refugees face, and the contributions they can make to their adopted country. This resource guide makes many generalizations, to avoid becoming overlong.

If you currently work with African immigrant elders or are planning to, remember that your first goal must always be to get to know each person and each group individually. The tools and advice provided in this guide will help you to prepare to work with different groups of African elderly immigrants. Understanding their experiences and perspectives will increase your capacity and competence.

My hope is that these stories and tips will help you to be more creative when applying your current practices to African elderly refugee individuals and groups in central Minnesota. Understanding the individual development of elderly immigrants as a general process will help you get better results while using fewer resources.

Resource Guide for Service Providers

Who is this guide designed for?

The resource guide may be used by a variety of audiences, and can be tailored to the interests and educational backgrounds of service providers. The objective of the resource guide is to reach a broad cross-section of central Minnesota's service providers.

Some of the groups who may benefit from the resource guide:

- Service providers including those who work with family violence, drug addiction, mental health, housing, and transportation.
- Professionals such as doctors, dentists, pharmacists, bankers, lawyers, and police officers.
- Community leaders.

- "Gatekeepers" (people who have regular contact with older adults, e.g., postal workers, business operators, and landlords); employers of people caring for older adults at home.
- Staff at senior centers.
- Crisis line and telephone referral volunteers.
- Staff and management at long-term care facilities or in emergency care settings.
- Public policy makers.
- Religious leaders.

The appendix includes contact information and details for selected organizations, publications, and websites. The format of the resource guide is intended to allow for constant updating by individual users as new resources are generated. This resource guide can be used in conjunction with other resources already available.

The Role of the Community in Helping African Immigrant Elders

The central Minnesota community can provide support for African immigrant elders by assisting with transportation, delivering meals at home, visiting homemakers or home nursing care, financial or legal advice, counseling, and day programs. Many of these services may not be available in rural or isolated communities. In those cases, the role of supporting African immigrant elders may fall on staff and volunteers from public health clinics, community centers or religious organizations.

African Immigrant Refugees' Experience in the United States

I mmigrant refugees often flee their homes with no time for preparation. They leave behind almost everything, including professional documents, photographs, and other valuable items. Far worse, they often leave behind family members. Immigrant refugees often do not trust people other than family members and close friends. Immigrant refugees are people without homes. Eventually, after many years in refugee camps, they receive permission to settle in the United States and begin adapting to a new culture and a new language.

Values and Beliefs

I t is often difficult to recognize the effect traditional beliefs have on professional and personal relationships. It is difficult to admit to ourselves that we have certain biases. Religious service providers dealing with African immigrant elders can let personal values affect their responses to clients. A person's value system affects decision-making, and service providers need to recognize and reconcile their values with their responsibilities. This may require a change in deep-seated attitudes.

African Christianity

The growth of Christianity in Africa in recent years has been spectacular. The availability and appeal of the Bible has been identified as a major contributor to the phenomenal growth of Christianity in Africa. Given the oral tradition of African Christians and the literary tradition the Bible represents, the interaction between the Bible and culture in African Christianity is intriguing. Christian social service providers in central Minnesota must help Christian elder refugees resolve the disconnect between the Bible and African cultures.

This part of the book will assist service providers to understand how to help individual elder refugees adjust to their new lives and accomplish their goals.

In this section, service providers will have an opportunity to assess African immigrant elder's major challenges. In addition, this chapter will provides some concrete advice for institutions, government agencies, nonprofits, funders, and religious corporations that wish to better serve refugees communities.

Major Challenges

The major challenges confronting African elderly immigrants are:

- Weather
- Loss
- Lack of Transportation
- Health Problems
- Language Barriers

- Cultural Competency
- Dress in Muslim Tradition
- Food
- Time
- Touch and Its Social Implications
- Handshakes or Greetings
- The Use of the Left Hand
- Music

- Respect for Older People
- Eye Contact
- Culture Shock

Weather

Coping with major change in climate is a big adjustment for new refugees at the arrival stage, many of whom come from much warmer places. Some elders are excited to see and touch snow for the first time in their lives. I remember when my plane left Ghana in 2003, it was 75°F; when I arrived at the Minneapolis/ Saint Paul international airport, it was −32°F. I had not prepared for this kind of frigid weather. One of my friends provided a jacket for me. But even my borrowed winter jacket was not meant for that temperature. Climate was the first of many differences I had to adapt to.

Loss

S ome African immigrant elders feel a sense of loss after arrival. This sense of loss is compounded by social isolation. New African immigrant elders face language and cultural barriers. Some new African immigrant elders live in apartments surrounded by people from cultures other than their own. Some are afraid of using public transportation because they fear getting lost. In addition, they often do not read or speak English, so written signs and assistance from English-only speakers cannot be understood.

Lack of Transportation

I n their home countries, some African immigrant elders traveled by foot from one village to another. While others lived in large cities, African immigrant elders still have problems negotiating new transportation systems. Language and communication barriers also limit their ability to get a driver's license, read signs, or communicate with others.

Having one's own transportation or knowing how to use public transportation helps African immigrant elders succeed. Sometimes elders have to depend on their children or friends whenever they want to go to somewhere. What happens if their children work two or three jobs and have no time for their parents' needs? In winter, elders often have no choice but to stay home, which leads to boredom and isolation; both causes of depression among the African immigrant elder population. Service providers should teach elders how to use public transit.

Health Problems

H ealth problems related to a lack of food, medicine, and water are common among elderly immigrants. Refugees often suffer from depression as a result of removal, loss, or physical torture. Physical and mental health problems often accompany a refugee to their new homeland. Many Somali elders suffer from diabetes due to an inability to digest refined sugars and other foods and a lack of exercise. Some elderly immigrants do not want to share their health problems with people other than family members, including doctors. Others have never visited doctors, or years have passed since their last checkup. Others do not believe in Western medicine, and have their own systems of medicine. Sometimes the health care system does not provide elder immigrants with accessible services, either linguistically or culturally. Some diseases did not exist in the refugees' homeland. In some cases, a refugee's culture might have a different explanation for a given illness, and this can increase misunderstanding.

Language Barriers

L anguage barriers often prevent elderly immigrants and the service providers who help them from understanding each other. Some elderly immigrants simply have not yet learned to communicate effectively in English. Many service providers likely speak one language—a language problem of their own. Both elderly immigrants and Americans have language difficulties that prevent them from working effectively together. The elderly immigrants often must learn how to understand people who speak English with an accent.

Cultural Competency

E very human being is a member of one or more cultures. These cultures influence an individual's beliefs, practices, behaviors, and personality. A person who has cultural competency has specific knowledge of other people's cultures, backgrounds, values, and beliefs, as well as skill in obtaining cultural knowledge which he or she lacks (Kohls, 1996).

Cultural competency helps eliminate, overcome, or reduce cultural barriers when working with diverse groups. For instance, most Somalis, Ethiopians, and Sudanese share the same language, religion, and culture, but they are divided into groups by a deeply-rooted clan structure. Because of deep clan divisions, a person who works with one group of elderly refugees and then tries to generalize his or her experience to apply to all can meet with devastating failure. In general, cultural differences often lead to misunderstanding or misinterpretation of messages between people of different cultures. One's culture encodes specific nonverbal behaviors or body languages, which represent specific thoughts, feelings, and meanings. Different interpretations of body language are among the most difficult problems in any cross-cultural communication.

Dress in Muslim Tradition

I n Islamic tradition, dress is important for Somali women and men. For example, women are expected to wear *hijab*, a dress that covers the body except for the hands and face. Men should also wear clothes that cover the body between waist and knees according to tradition. Both sexes are to start dressing this way when they are between seven and nine years old.

Food

Why is food so important for new elderly immigrants? Food can be a major issue for new arrivals. The human body adapts to food from a particular locale. In the United States, many food portions are very large and the diet has a lot of fat, sugar, and salt. The result of an American diet for some immigrants is an increase in obesity and related diseases such as diabetes.

Food is one of the important elements of Muslim culture and religion. Islamic tradition prohibits the consumption of pork or alcohol. The most common foods in Muslim tradition include rice, beef, beans, and goat meat.

Different Concepts of Time

Time concepts vary widely from one culture to the next. Americans who do not have experience with elderly immigrants often grow impatient with what they perceive as wasted time. Here Americans need to understand different approaches to time. Elderly refugees also ought to learn and adapt the attitudes, behaviors, and practices of American people relating to time. Most American people tend to perceive time as a linear movement. In contrast, most elderly African immigrant do not use clocks or calendars as important determinants of their actions and priorities. They perceive time as a circular movement, and believe that time will come back tomorrow, next season, or next year. Service providers must remember that each individual and each group of people is different. There may be a need for providers to know their clients' attitude toward time and adjust their work processes accordingly.

Touch and Its Social Implications

Some Americans are uncomfortable with touching among non-family members. For some Africans, greetings that include hugs or kisses, along with touching, generally between the same sexes during conversation, are standard ways to convey connection. These actions can cause discomfort and negative reactions in cultures that are not touch-oriented, such as the case with Muslim women.

Handshakes or Greetings

Handshakes are recognized as a standard means of greeting throughout the world. How people shake hands however, can carry unintended meanings. In the Muslim culture, handshakes across gender are not acceptable except between spouses. Some elderly Muslims may have difficulties when they meet Americans who do not know the Muslim tradition. They often cannot explain this matter because of language barriers.

Greetings are very important in Africa. When a person fails to greet, African elders say he is not friendly or not polite. Such a person has no respect for others, or maybe he has not been trained well by his parents. Greetings bring people together. In Africa, a person does not greet only those he knows. A good African greets anybody, whether he is familiar or not. When a younger person greets an older person, the older responds and offers a polite inquiry regarding the greeter's health. Usually younger people do not ask older people such questions, unless they know the older person is not well.

Every greeting has a response. The greetings and the responses bring the two people closer together. Greetings are important in bringing peace between people. When two people quarrel, older people try to bring them together. They make sure the two people shake hands and greet each other any time they meet.

The Use of the Left Hand

In Africa, it is generally good to greet or shake hands with the right hand, and not the left hand. Africans do not use the left hand to do anything, especially in the sight of an older person. African elders believe that the left hand is not clean. It is taboo in West Africa to use the left hand to point something out to people, or make a sign to call people. If they must use the left hand because the right hand is busy, they are expected to apologize and explain why using the left hand was necessary.

Music

African people love music. They show their feelings and actions through songs, drumming, and dancing. You can tell whether an African is happy or sad when he sings or dances. Most African songs are accompanied with drumming and dancing. Some are sung on occasions such as funerals, festivals, or marriages. Others are sung as part of ritual storytelling. Some traditional African jobs have songs that go with them. Fishermen, for example, enjoy pulling their nets with music, and some farmers sing while weeding.

Respect for Older People

In some African societies, a young person wearing a hat or cap must remove their headwear when greeting elders. When entering the rooms of an elder, young people are expected to remove their sandals. These are just two examples of honoring one's elders, both important to know when working with African immigrants. Another example: when adults are conversing, children are not allowed to take part unless they are invited to do so. Children should also note that it is good for them to give their seats to adults when necessary. Children must help adults, especially the old men and women, whenever possible. For example, when children see adults carrying loads, they are expected to help them.

Eye Contact

Eye contact is understood to indicate interest and forthrightness among most Americans. But in Africa, avoidance of direct and prolonged eye contact is generally a sign of respect. Misinterpretation of the meaning of eye contact can lead to serious misunderstandings between people of different cultures.

Culture Shock

Culture shock is a common problem that almost every new refugee faces. There are few immigrant refugees who realize the extent of the challenge of culture shock. Most new immigrants do not anticipate shock or understand that it can come from many factors, such as language, weather, food, and culture. Sometimes culture shock causes depression, and depression can exacerbate other problems.

Summary

The foregoing categories are broad sketches of the challenges that face African immigrant elders to central Minnesota. If elders can find solutions as they adjust to a new culture, they can advance personally and professionally. The nature of one's individual challenges are diverse and subtle, and depend on the age, educational background, services received, family support, and home culture of a new arrival. For this reason, no single set of guidelines applies to their experiences or the kinds of help they need. It is important to listen to and understand the individual stories, backgrounds, cultures, and needs of African immigrant elders. The central Minnesota community that receives them, and especially service providers, must learn about their challenges, assist them where possible, and come to understand new neighbors as the potential assets they are.

Appendix

Websites

Forced Migration

http://www.forcedmigration.org

An international site that offers lots of information about refugees and immigrants, from refugee laws to health issues of forced migration peoples, including children and elderly. This site links to other resources: journals; databases; academic research institutes; governmental, inter-governmental, and multilateral institutions; non-governmental agencies; and non-electronic resources. Forced Migration also has a bibliography to guide further reading.

International Thesaurus of Refugee Terminology

---

http://www.refugeethesaurus.org

Provides an online reference, and allows users to find more information on specific terms from an alphabetical display of terms, or to search for specific terms.

United States Citizenship and Immigration Services

---

http://www.uscis.gov

A United States government website hosting information for refugees and immigrants who resettle in the United States, including how to apply for green cards and for citizenship. It provides legal forms, guides, and information on benefits and relevant laws.

Organizations

Catholic Charities

Providing help, creating hope, serving all faiths, Catholic Charities is a non-profit organization, which advances the charitable and social mission of the Diocese of St. Cloud. This group builds communities, promotes family life, and enhances human dignity by providing quality human services meeting the physical, social, emotional, and spiritual needs of individuals and family of all faiths and beliefs.

Housing Management Services

Provides professional management to landlords and affordable housing to tenants. Catholic Charities Housing Management Services provides professional services to the landlords and tenants of low-income housing across central Minnesota. Their management team places an emphasis on respect for individual tenants. Catholic Charities advocates for tenants' rights, and facilitates the delivery of support services, especially the elderly.

Food Shelf

This organization makes available approximately a week's supply of food on a one-time-per-calendar-month basis, at no cost. First-time clients must provide identification for themselves and all members of their household and demonstrate proof of residence prior to receiving services. Proof of income is requested to determine eligibility.

Hours: Monday 9:00 AM to 6:00 PM; seniors (over the age of sixty) second and fourth Tuesdays 1:00 PM to 3:00 PM; Wednesday 9:00 AM to 8:00 PM; Friday 9:00 AM to noon

Financial Assistance

Financial assistance provides immediate, short-term assistance to families in financial crisis. Requests are evaluated on an individual basis. For elderly refugees, assistance can be provided to cover bus cards and apartment application fees.

Catholic Charities is an Equal Opportunity Service Provider to better help immigrant refugees.

Catholic Charities Contact Information

157 Roosevelt Road, Suite 200

St. Cloud, MN 56301

Telephone: (320) 229-4576

Toll-Free Telephone: (800) 830-8254

Fax: (320) 253-7464

Hours: Monday through Friday, 8:00 AM to 4:30 PM

http://www.ccstcloud.org

Lutheran Social Service

This Christian-affiliated social service provider serves all people regardless of race, color, creed, religion, sex, sexual orientation, disability, or age. This group is particularly interested in advocacy and human rights, community service, employment assistance, and helping refugees.

Contact Information:

Lutheran Social Service

22 Wilson Avenue NE, Suite 110

St. Cloud, MN 56301

Telephone: (320) 251-7700

Housing Redevelopment and Authority

The mission statement of HRA is to identify housing and development needs, implement programs to assist residents with low incomes, and facilitate development opportunities throughout the county.

Housing Redevelopment and Authority

720 West Germain, Suite 143

St. Cloud, MN 56301

Telephone: (320) 257-6630 or (320) 252-0880

Toll-Free Telephone: (800) 515-5253

Hands Across the World

Welcoming and assisting newly-arrived refugees and immigrants to the St. Cloud community, HATW provides a first contact for those lacking language or living skills necessary to thrive in the central Minnesota community.

Contact Information:

Hands Across the World

1605 Goettens Way, #206

St. Cloud, MN 56301

Telephone: (320) 230-0818

E-mail: handsacrosstheworld@astound.net

http://www.handsacrosstheworld.org

References

Abou El Fadl, K. (2002). *The place of tolerance in Islam*. Oxford: One World.

Abu-Lughod, J. (1989). *Before European hegemony: The World system* A.D. 1250–1350. New York: Oxford University Press.

Adamo, D. T. (1998). *Africa and the Africans in the Old Testament*. San Francisco: Christian Universities Press.

Adamo, D. T. (2000). *Africa and the New Testament*. Unpublished manuscript.

Ahmed, A. S. (1986). *Toward an Islamic anthropology: Definition, dogma, and directions*. Herndon, VA: International Institute of Islamic Thought.

Allen, J., Cochran, D., Dean, C., & Greene, J. (1989). *Networking bulletin: Empowerment and family support* (Vol. 1, Issue 1). Ithaca, NY: Cornell Empower Group.

Armstrong, K. (2002). *Islam: A short history*. New York: Modern Library.

Augsburger, D. W. (1986). *Pastoral counseling across cultures*. Philadelphia: Westminster.

Azoy, G. W. (2003). *Buzkashi: Game and power in Afghanistan* (Second ed.). Prospect Heights, IL: Waveland Press.

Ben-Jochannan, Y. (2002). *African origins of major Western religions.* New York: Alkebu-lan Books.

Bloom, M., & Fisher, J., (1982). *Evaluating practice: Guidelines for the accountable professional.* Englewood Cliffs, NJ: Prentice Hall.

Blythe, B., Briar, S., & Tripodi, T. (1994). *Direct practice research in human service agencies.* New York: Columbia University Press.

Born, D. (1980). "Psychological adaptation and development under acculturative stress: Toward a general model." *Social Science and Medicine, 3,* 529–547.

Bosch, D. (1995). *Dynamique de la mission chretienne: Histoire et avenir des modeles missionaries.* Paris and Geneva: Lome.

Buono, M. D., Urciuoli, O., & De Leo, D. (1998). "Quality of life and longevity. A study of centenarians." *Age and Aging, 27,* 1–12.

Callaway, B., & Creevy, L. (1994). *Women, religion, and politics in West Africa.* Boulder: Lynne Rienner.

Canedy, D. (2002, June 27). "Lifting veil for photo id goes too far, driver says." *New York Times,* p. A16.

Collins, P. M., Kayser, K., & Platt, S. (1994). "Conjoint marital therapy: A practitioner's approach to single-system evaluation." *Families in Society, 75,* 131–141.

Collins, P. M., Kayser, K., & Tourse, R. (1994). "Bridging the gaps: An interdependent model for educating accountable practitioners." *Journal of Social Work Education,* 30, 241–251.

Drachman, D. (1995). "Immigration statuses and their influence on service provision, access, and use." *Social Work,* 40, 188–197.

Dyal, J. A., & Dyal, R. Y. (1981). "Acculturation, stress and coping." *International Journal of Intercultural Relations,* 5, 301–328.

Ellison, C. W. (1983). "Spiritual well-being: Conceptualization and measurement." *Journal of Psychology and Theology,* 1(1), 330–340.

Esposito, J. L. (1998). *Islam: The straight path* (Third ed.). New York. Oxford University Press.

Fulmer, T. T., & O'Malley, T. A. (1987). *Inadequate care of the elderly: A health care perspective on abuse and neglect.* New York: Springer.

Furnhan, A., & Bochner, S. (1986). *Cultural shock: Psychological reactions to unfamiliar environments.* New York: Methuen.

Geffre, C. (2006). *De Babel a Pentecote: Essais de theologie interreligieuse.* Paris: CERF.

Getui, M., Holter, K., & Zinkuratire, V. (2001). *Interpreting the Old Testament in Africa.* New York: Oxford.

Hickson, J., Housley, W., & Wages, D. (2000). "Counselors' perceptions of spirituality in the therapeutic process." *Counseling and Values,* 45, 1–16.

Hussain, A., Olson, R., & Qureshi, J. (1984). *Orientalism, Islam, and Islamists.* Brattleboro, VT: Amana Books.

Jacob, A. G. (1994). "Social integration of Salvadoran refugees." *Social Work,* 39, 307–312.

Kinkupu, S. (2005). *Les defis de l'evangelisation dans l'Afrique contemporaine.* Paris: Karthala.

Koenig, H. G., (2000). "Religion, spirituality, and medicine: Application to clinical practice." *The Journal of the American Medical Association,* 284, 1–4.

Kohls, L. R. (1996). *Survival kit for overseas living.* Maine: Intercultural Press, Inc.

Lazarus, R. S., & Folkman, S. (1984). *Stress, appraisal, and coping.* New York: Springer.

Longatan, N. (2008). *Culture shock and cross-cultural adjustment.* Philippines: Author.

Maher, J. (1999). "The five secrets of centenarians." *Anti-Aging Longevity News.*

Mbiti, J. S. (1981). *African religions and philosophy.* New York: Doubleday.

Mbiti, J. S. (2000). *African religions and culture.* New York: Doubleday.

Nawwab, N. I. (1992). "The journal of a lifetime." *Aramco World,* 43(4), 27–35.

O'Keefe, J. (2000). *A heart healthy lifestyle: How to live 100 years, be youthful, vigorous, healthy, and happy for a lifetime.* Kansas City, MO: Author.

New Oxford American Dictionary (2005), p. 346.

Padilla, A. M. (Ed.). (1980). *Acculturation: Theory, models, and some new findings.* Boulder, CO: Westview Press.

Padilla, A. M., Alvarez, M., & Lindholm, K. (1986). "Generational status and personality factors as predictors of stress in students." *Hispanic Journal of Behavioral Sciences*, 8, 275–288.

Parachin, V. M. (1994). "Facts of life: A dozen ways to live longer and better." *American Fitness*, 12, 1–4

Perls, T. T., & Silver, M. H. (1996). *Living to 100: Lessons in living to your maximum potential at any age.* New York: Basic Books.

Richardson, A. A. (1987). "Theory and method for the psychological study of assimilation." *International Migration Review*, 2, 3–30.

Routhier, G. (1993). *La reception d'un concile.* Paris: CERF.

United Nations. (2006). *Analytical report. Volume 3 of World Population Prospects: The 2004 revision.* New York: United Nations.

United States Bureau of the Census. (2000). *Populations of the United States by age, sex, race, and African origin.* 1995 to 2050: Current population reports (pp. 25–1130). Washington, DC: United States Government Printing Office.

United States Department of Justice. (1993). *1992 statistical yearbook of the immigration and naturalization service.* Washington, DC: Author.

Winter, A. (2000). *Who's 100 and why.* Retrieved from http://www.adlercentenarians.com.

www.ingramcontent.com/pod-product-compliance
Lightning Source LLC
Chambersburg PA
CBHW021256280526
45784CB00005B/2394